SONGS OF THE HEART

CHEENA PURI

Copyright © Cheena Puri
All Rights Reserved.

I dedicate this book to my parents Mahinder Pal Puri and Shashi Lata Puri who are a great source of encouragement in all my endeavours . My father-in-law Professor Harbhagwan Miglani who keeps motivating me with his spiritual discourses . My husband Dr Vivek Miglani who overly appreciated my manuscripts that made me wonder if it was a credit to my writings or an indicaton of his non- literary background. My sisters Prerna Kumar and Nishtha Puri and my brothers-in-law, Sanjay Kumar and Shashi Kiran who have been an inspiration to me for their exemplary pursuits and excellence in their respective fields. Ram , Kartikeya and Naraini the three pearls of our family who always leave me awe struck with their amazing combination of innocence and maturity.

Contents

Preface

Thinking retrospectively on when and how I started writing poems I recall how as a child I used to pen down few liners in rhyming scheme on small bits of paper and collect them in a box. As I grew older the rhyming schemes and sing song forms of my poems were replaced by blank verse. The subject matter also changed its garb from the child like wonder on the starry nights, awe srtuck twinkle in the eyes on watching fluttering butterflies to the inner realm of confusing forms . As Shelley beautifuly wrote in *To a Skylark*, "Our sweetest songs are those that tell of saddest thought", many of my poems spring from the incomprehsible upsurge of emotions of myriad shades. Two worlds exist in one mind ,one created by the yearnings of the heart , pure and blissful and the other of the shattering images moving through the maze called life.

Acknowledgements

My gratitude to my family and friends who spurred me on to keep writing .

Prologue

The feelings , the sensations , the innumerale waves crashing on the shore of the heart are too complex, deep, immeasurale and intangible.To capture these subtleties and give them form is Art. Poetry is one of the genres of literary art that brings to life the unexpressible and fleeting forms and images of human experience and thought.

Songs of the Heart

Contents

CONTENTS

1. The Resurrection

There lies in every heart a child
Innocent, pure, carefree and free of vile

As we grow in years
We lose touch with that tiny hand
There comes in between the child and the man
A demon.
A demon that feeds on hatred, envy, evil and discontent.

As the demon grows within us,
We move away and away from the child -
The symbol of purity, wonder and of true happiness.
We run after more and more and more
But get nothing but the void.
For what we lose is the simple pleasure of life-
Purity of a smile, of laughter, of tears and of
Simple joys- which form the essence of life

Only if we could resurrect the buried child
The demon could be exorcised,
And we be saved from
The dismal sorrows of life.

2. Phoenix

I am a Phoenix bird,
Each time I die, I get a new birth.
I have died many times, but only to rise each time from my
ashes.

It is not easy to die.
It is very painful to burn in the fire of hell.
It takes a long dreary time to take a new birth.

The death is slow …..
Piercing!
The tunnel of darkness is long, very long….
Hope feeble, steps languid with ache.

But I have to move on
And I do keep moving
Because I am a Phoenix bird –
Destined to be born anew from my ashes.

And with every birth, is born in me
A new self – stronger, surer, wiser and deeper
That soars higher and higher…….
Nearer to the birth-giver.

3. Winter

The advent of winter – like something pleasant tinkling your
senses
And warming your heart.
A bright twinkling in your eyes
Heralding
The waves from far off lands:
Forgotten moments from the past,
Of forgone years, of playfulness,
Childhood days of carefreeness.
The sniff of winter air
Mingled with jubilant moisture.
The misty air that numbs the conscious – the over conscious
brain of summer heat,
And transports to a world of slumber…. active slumber!!
Dewy air that induces forgetfulness,
Of the acute presence of reality,
And sleepily delivers to the pleasantness of childhood days.

4. Aroma

The escapades for savouring the aroma of freedom
Amidst the turmoil of life's unexplainable twists
Moments which were the only means to be oneself —and breathe
life.
The precious moments snatched from the barred existence:
The pearls of laughter as the purity of pearls
The joy of freedom as the sky full of birds
The warmth of love and togetherness

As the brightness of the Sun.

To grab the fresh breath of life
To fly with the refreshing cool breeze
To savour the aroma brewing from the essence of one's true, free
being.

5. Summer

The advent of summer – Like someone
Crudely shaking you out of the winter dreaminess
Back to the dullness of heat.
Out of the empty, dry, void air,
The tiny black monsters-
Flying distances from the mustard fields
Choking your mouth and blinding your eyes and
Crudely announcing…. the beginning of long, dreary summer
days:
The slow pace of life,
as the slowly moving dull lengthy days.
Dragging with it the dark shadows,
Gloomy images and morbid reflections of the past.

6. Ennui

Vacuum......narrowing of one's circle, circle of love and
companionship.
The unveiling of the cruder and malicious aspects of relations
once felt so pure, so joyful.
Breaking up of past images of bonding......
All blown into the air as chimeras.
Images of people now gone away, away into the alley of
indifference.....
To haunt, to howl in the emptiness within.
The void and the vacuum
Of being in a world full of people,
Of relations so distant and empty.
The piercing ennui of being with oneself
sans any pleasant picture of the past
Boredom in the present
Indefiniteness in the future.

7. Vision

Cool breeze blowing,
Caressing the cold cheeks.
Glint of cheer in the twinkling eyes.
The bubbly, clear blue stream flowing ,
And under its transparent glean
The pebbles brown and shining,
Fishes criss crossing.
Lying pondering on the hammock swing
Capturing through the inward eye
the exhilaration of flowing with the heavenly breeze,
Climbing high on the snow clad mountains.....
Flying with the birds in the blue, blue, deep blue expansive sky
The Bliss of joy!!!
Lets complete the pleasant vision
with savoring aroma of hot coffee
and vanish to the magical fictional world
Wearing wings of time to far off lands.

8. Stroll

Strolling in the early morn
On the winding, meandering roads……
Going up and then coming down.
The sea beyond,
The misty, hazy, reddish yellow trees
The orangish- red sky…
All greedily gulped in by the starving mind, the pining eyes
Watching with wonder
The break of dawn on a morning stroll.

9. Flux

Relations are always in a flux....
always changing their colour ,
and the shades from white to grey to black...to grey
It is difficult to grasp the true essence ...
Still amidst the dark shades of anger, clashes, distance of
indifference
Something still remains to bind one another.

10. Hurdle Race

Life is like a hurdle race…..
Spanned with bumps big and small
And they end with the end of life…
Just like in the race they stop with the finishing line.

• 14 •

11. The path to Victory

God makes his children learn the lessons of life
Through their encounter with adversities, trials and strives-
Unpleasant and irking to mind.
Two paths seem to be before us
One is easy to walk on unthinking …un-steered,
Flowing with the tide
Losing your being to the troubled time.
The other is difficult to walk on
Requires firm feet to hold on to your pride
To call upon your strongest being,
Bringing to fore your mettle, and shine.
Watch closely, God purposely opens a freedom of choice
It is always easy to follow the path of escape
But hold on, don't let go off the path of real gain.
Walk on till you win over your weaker frame.
Purge yourself of the Excess!!
Keep the essence …Weed away the superficial, the insignificant
The futile.
Make a garden of your life.

12. Danger-Line

Don't just don't cross the danger line.
There is fire, storm, earthquake, and flood on the other side.
There the floor is too shaky for your too weak feet.
You will stumble, you'll fall.
Hold on here, here the ground is firm and hard.
The wind is silent. The waves calm.
The cinders cold – having spent their passion long.
Oh Yes! , I know here you have to stick to the ground.
You can't fly.
But why do you want to fly?
The wings of Icarus that carry you to the sky ….will soon melt
with the heat of the sun,

And you will fall …fall a great height
That will crumble you and your spirit alike.
So don't, just cross the danger line.

13. The Indian Rail

The mesmerizing sound of the whistle of the Indian rail,
Rushing forward on its trail.
The expanse of mud hills on either side
of the steamy soldier with its unwavering and ardent gaze,
Focused to reach its destination in haste.
Gushing forward wearing the fervent red and black cloak,
Donning its majestic armour with its rumbling roar.
It didn't know someone is enchanted by its grace and rushes out
to get a glimpse of its shooting pace.

Will you hold on for some time and let me absorb your heroic
demeanor for a while!!!
To keep your image a bit longer on my mind's frame.
But not to halt, not to break and not to look back is its shining
fate.

14. Grow Up Now!!

Having lived some four scores and one,
Was wondering have I grown up now??
Grown not just in years but in my world of thoughts.
Looking back at my long stumbling journey - from a dreamy
adolescent to a half-baked adult.....
Meandering through roads of miseries,
Passions uncontrolled and unexplained woes of heart,
Moving on, from the disturbing divide between reason and
emotions,
Rising through churning whirlpools
Of confusing images of self and others.
I tapped on my shoulder for I thought
I could now erase past pains with balm of wisdom newly found!!
So have I now landed on the calm ground?
Have I come closer to having a grip on myself?
Have I found myself and can I rely on the path leading forward?
Feeling complacent that now I could steer through the plains and
valleys alike
I said to myself with some pride , "Yes I have"!!
Kept Floating like a feather with a sense of self assurance for
some while .....

But Lo! My flight could not sustain long,
Unable to balance in the crashing waves
Of harsh words and circumstantial foes
Staggering to rise, I say to Myself " Grow up Now"!!.

15. Trial Room

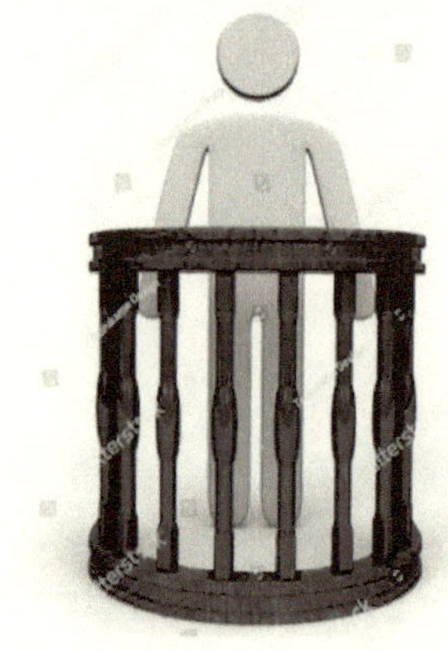

When and why and how I was put in the witness box I had no clue.
I was perplexed as I was questioned for wrongs I didn't do. How could I defend myself when the jury was conducting a trial
Which needed no proof of innocence; all pleas were looked upon with wide angry eyes,
For I was already sentenced guilty in the jury's mind.
The trial didn't require justifications, no explanations; no appeals could pierce the jury walls,
As this court room only conducted one way trials…

*Where the judge judged on the basis of prejudices and
convictions of own.
I only wondered on the elusive nature of the crime
I committed no murder, no theft, and no forgery
I was only too naïve to play the game of being what I was not
inside
Not being able to enact the image of and play pretense to judge's
whims
And cunningly to get the control of judge in due time .
My only crime was I couldn't be who I was not inside.*

16. On Freedom

Be the bird....Fly on
fly high up in the open sky!
Away, away from the chores.....chains,
Away to the world of peace, love freedom and joy,
With windy waves, rain water, away, away into the sky

9 7 9 8 8 8 6 8 4 7 3 6 9